ON STARRY THIGHS

SENSUAL AND SACRED POETRY

On Starry Thighs

Sensual and Sacred Poetry

By Lee Harrington

Mystic Productions Press

© 2015 – Mystic Productions Press
www.MysticProductionsPress.com
411 W. Northern Lights Blvd.
Anchorage, AK 99503

By Lee Harrington
www.PassionAndSoul.com

All artwork by Abby Helasdottir
abby.gydja.com

Special thanks to Deborah Addington
www.DeborahAddington.com

ISBN: 978-0-9778727-6-3

TABLE OF CONTENTS

INTRODUCTION

Poetry is a secret prayer, a passion, an obsession. It begins as love letters and displays of lust. It bubbles to the surface as a form of pain processing or erupts like flames of devotion. Oracular downloads spring up like blossoms or feel like fingernails caught violently under a vice grip.

This collection of work covers nearly twenty years of poetic creation. Some are barely touched from when they first came into being, while others have been worked and re-worked so many times that they are barely recognizable from when they came screaming from the womb of creativity.

They are slices from my life or from the lives of the divinities I have been blessed to embody. They are gifts of inspiration from (and to) my lovers and beloved friends over the years, including my lover who is myself.

They are my vulnerable heart laid bare.

I offer this book as a supplication, my dusty knees grinding into the hearth of mystery. It includes specific devotional prayers to a variety of deities, but it also holds a collection of erotic delight as well. It holds tales of my suffering and struggles with the hope that they will reach one heart to say "I am not alone, for they have walked this road as well."

Will you hold my hand and walk this winding path at my side? It would be my honor to offer this liturgy with you as my witness. In turn I will hold space for your invocation of dirty dreams and hidden fears. Let these pages open up their arms and provide a safe space for you. They will not judge your veiled anguish and covert pleasures.

At the end of the day, faith and desire are flip sides of the same coin, dishes best served in the same meal. Both call for passion, both call for soul. All of these things are mine; by handing this work to you, they become yours as well.

Blessed be.

Yours in Passion and Soul,

> Lee Harrington
> June 2015
> Anchorage, Alaska, USA

THE BOOK OF ORACLES

...the world foretold

Temple within temple I welcome you
Temple within temple, protections cast
We turn
We spin
Writhing tentacles, writhing beasts
Opening under the hallowed words
Welcomed under the temple eye

How does one reflect back
Two days three nights work
In words where you are there lapping at my thigh?

I hand you my key
Bind blood to blood, flesh to flesh
Drinking deep
Words flowing like the water you are
Drinking deep
Eye to eye and heart to heart
Welcomed under the temple eye

Measure me by weights and scales
Measure me by my deeds and reach
Measure me as we drink deep and measure once more
Welcomed under the temple eye

Open me
into eternity
We glimpse the water
Finding we already knew how to dance

TEMPLE ORACLE

I speak through the fractured mouths of a thousand caves
shining brilliantly in the darkness
reaching out into time
let me touch upon the never was
the always must be

Visions come to touch my tongue
a stumbling river
rumbling across the stones of a crumbling edifice
forgotten walls
inlaid with the stories of fate
forgotten to poisoned fingers and linen ligaments

Yesterday we foretold a tale of broken hearts
needful gods lapping at their ancient wounds
voices heavy with rumors
over and over again
echoing across the empty plains

Here we find ourselves
find myself shuddering at your touch
divinity reached its voice out through piercing screams
speaking hear my words
here my words
torn open like a wound

Turn once more to the temple oracle
face the dreams we dared not dream
once more we turn
answering the call
of what might be once more

STARRY GODDESS

Wrinkles within wrinkles
a star in each fold
Impossibly young
Beyond all reproach
Eternally all ages
black and starry skin
You arc overhead
You

Once upon a time
that was a time before time
there was nothing except Her.

Floating in the formless void
in a nothingness
in a black deeper than a sigh
She floated eternal in Herself.

She
Star Goddess
Starry Goddess
blacker than a sigh.

Floating in the formless void
in a time before time
the Starry Goddess gazed upon a mirror.

From the nothingness She watched Herself
saw Herself
floating eternal in Herself.

And She liked what She saw.

She breathed into Herself
She opened Her eyes to the majesty of Herself
the beauty of Herself
the grace of Herself
and became enamored.

In the time before time
with nothing but Herself and the mirror that reflected Her back
She was enthralled.

She was delicious and delighted.

Her starry thighs and gasps
echoed against one another
in the void that was blacker than a sigh.

Her skin
blacker than a sigh
took in Her caresses
and caressed Her in return.

Lover of self
self-lover
lover Starry Goddess sighed.

She roared and bucked against the blackness.

She felt Herself full of potential
full of bliss
full of truth and possibilities.

She tensed up
arched Her back
Her long star-filled locks flowing down Her body.

She arched and cried out
let fly the stars from Her being.

In Her waves came forth the constellations.
In Her waves came forth the nebulas and galaxies.
In Her waves came forth the dust and dreams.
In Her waves She came and we came forth.

Once upon a time
in a time before time
She floated in the formless void.

In a nothingness
in a black deeper than a sigh
She floated eternal in Herself.

Until She sighed
She moaned
gazing into the mirror.

Until She came
and we came forth.

Self-love is an act of creation.
Each caress an act of devotion.
Starry Goddess, Star Goddess...

Let kisses fall upon flesh peering in the mirror of self.
Let hands stroke and probe knowing this act to be sacred.

Giving self to self
in a time between times.

Giving birth to reality
with every sigh.

SYBILLINE

Flowing force of nature
you became my prophetess
my speaker of truths

Who was I to deny
the substance of your burning psyche
passions unfolding under an open sky

You let me access the crypt
step by step down into you
languid in our mysteries

Who was I to dream
forgotten shadows of the future
echoed apparitions of the past

Touched by Cassandra
I needed you
but never believed you

Dancing towards tomorrow
I wanted you
but never heeded your call

SEPULTURE

You spoke of fantastical truths
mechanized dervishes and apocalyptic trust
falling from a fertile tongue

I listened rapt and ravenous
needful of something to believe in
after a past laid to waste

Lurid possibilities escaped
from your enticing tattered tales
and I believed every one

Stories of the future were spun
gobbled up in raging hunger
never questioning what they meant to me

My ears needed each syllable
each word murmured from a fevered sight
clinging to tomorrows rambling rust

But by believing in you
I cast myself in and down
through pages of prose passionately writ

What has never happened
dreamed dry my wells
eclipsing the world around me

What never will be has left me blind
to what is before my eyes
beauty lost to your story book suffering

The trance takes me in
pages flip one by one
as the world passes me by

Two fingers slide in
as I push back
against my identity

ORACLE

Let me be your Pythia
your temple oracle
breathing deep
the air
at Delphi

I would woo Apollo's secrets
from his molten lips
to give you all
the world
and its riches

Sing into my devoted eyes
steal my heart away
bleed me dry of
the essence
of life

I hand over the future
give over the past
secrets whispered from
the fire
inside

Outside the holy city
beyond the marble gate
I wait for you
the truth
unfolding

It will all come true
every word I spoke
every word you never said
to me my love
every word
you never said
to me

SOLVE

I wipe the slate clean
of our violent beauty
the passions we never held

Hundreds of stars in your palm
offered up to me
inhaling the universe in a premonition

The smiles we never had
glimmer in your need
gifts for me alone

We untangle
thin strands that never mattered
as lightness descends

Getting started is the hardest part
when we speak
we speak of miracles.

The touching points of deity upon our lives
a breath
a light switch
a powering on from somewhere
a gift.

If I were to pronounce you a miracle
what would you say?

Thousands of switches and connections
thrown into chorus to bring you here
to me.

A laugh
a sigh
a tear rolls down rather than crying out
YES this
Yes
this miracle.

A miracle forgotten like a light switch
taken for granted
thousands of miles away
water rumbles
through metal arteries
and pvc veins

the charge of our essence
pours through fine lines
held up by giants across the land
to bring us this prayer
this miracle.

We speak of miracles
yet marvel
that the most noble
powerful
profound
are those we do not notice
every day of our lives.

DODONA

In sacred Dodona
mud under foot
waving beech leaves
limbs reaching down

Mud under foot
whispers between branches
of the visions thrown
like a fisherman's net

Whispers between branches
truths of 10,000 years
beloved Goddess
dancing in dreams

Truths of 10,000 years
every priest before
swaying under prophecy
as twigs snap and writhe

Every priest before
hungry for blessings
eternal children
feet dirty with the truth

Hungry for blessings
shining long before Delphi
the oldest of oracles
sacred Dodona

Let forth the dappled holy light
of trees upon your sleeping skin
leaves scattered like Cumae visions
on dreaming ageless flesh

Last night we were bathed in reverie
paths we have not yet taken
and lovers not yet taken to bed
finding hope between our lips

You rode atop me charging prayers
cum soaked benedictions to tomorrow
each inhalation echoing lust
shuddering at my touch

Longing for our blessings born
of sun and aching forms below
screaming in our yet to be
toes curling as shallow breaths ring pure

What is a prayer but a noble truth
lit with will and desperately bound
palm to palm and cock to cock
singing out to be made true

It's not going to be okay
be what it was
be what yesterday whispered on the winds.

We once were comfortable
yesterday breathing deep our security
but life has been upended
cast by Fortuna at the gambling table.

I keep being told it will be okay
be what it was
be bold and beautiful under a mid-day sun.

I stare into empty eyes before me
solemn eyes raw from too many tears
shoulders up to ears that heard too many lies.

It will not be the same
never the same as we skirt across
the rim of the earth's edge into blackness.

The plagues have come
locusts and frogs from above
and I am sick of hearing that it will all be okay.

I am sick of reassurance
sick of the smiling painted masks
repeating again and again the same lines.

This tale will weave its way
along a path through shadow and loss
but it will never be the same.
Our tale will spin from here
into what it *will* be
into what tomorrow will whisper on the winds.

What would I change of myself
if destiny spun,
woven by my hand

Tomorrow's truths would untangle
across my calloused fingers
wyrd journeys knotted into the mystery

If each dream
were true from my tongue
what would I do

If each knowing fable
were unchangeable
yet wrought from my form

Unable to change
the potential for shame
growing with the warp

Embarrassed by each step
down the road
led to by the weft

Would I learn
what we each find
down the broken trail of faith

Knowing what will come
I ask if the web is woven
darker for this exposure

If love be seen broken
would I could I fight
for it to be held fast

Or would I knot up
inside and out
on the loom

tangles around
the shuttle of hope
lines left
        dangling

KNEELING FLAMES

Twin stars knee to knee
lotus prayers on carpeted dreams
an easy breath in
fingers clasp
and into the shadow descend

White drapes the Lady
while black drapes the Lord
the candlelit path awaits

White drapes the future
while black drapes the past
the candle lit path awaits

She kneels she kneels
At his foot and at his side
Grace and beauty
Devotion and love

Lifetimes unfold with the current
who cares about past lives
if today is left unseen

A hound at his side
A mother holding tight
A sacrifice
A lover
A child
A patchwork of clay

White and black whirl back
from light and echoing drums
guardian and journeyer
holding hands in the quest

Through myriad forms
through feasts and prayers
silent seated being
ecstatic moans airborne
and hair laying on the floor

White and black
kneeling before the flame
twin stars
held firm in each others arms

We walk
together
to the gate of possibilities
singing
know thyself
know thyself
to the winds

Open eyed
together
before the ashen altar
laying wreathes
burning incense
to the empty longing
of passions past

One stick for romance
one stick for fears
two sticks for hope
and two sticks for tears
as the clouds
rise up
to the heavens

Winds whisper back
wafting scents of truth
tears
future storms
on the horizon
unkind words shed
tears from a falling rage

So much need
stands
between our four empty arms
trembling
smoke ascending
in waves
until we crash

Until I turn to you
whispering
am I
your self-fulfilling
prophecy
your sacred error
your forgotten dream

Until you turn to me
whispering
words I will never hear
as we walk away
together
eternally apart
forever at the gate

THE BOOK OF WINGS

...the world ecstatic

He Dances

(for Melek Ta'us)

he dances with outspread wings
wheeling in the circles of my footsteps
dancing open
spinning me.
I breathe in the dance as he exposes me
naked in the circle of his majestic wings
reeling footsteps
of my dance
the ringing in my ears echo his desire
a ring of our footsteps lifting us up
quaking the ground
ancient rhythms of his memory
rising from lush valleys to endless stars
our eyes and hearts unveiled
he burns as he dances
writhing amongst flaming feathers
skin shakes and shivers
the rush of wind and eternity
burning away despair
emptying in ecstasy.
back on earth my spine is heavy
settling into my flesh once more
finding my way
out of his feathered embrace
his fiery claws release me
blue reaching deep and peeling back
drawing away

out of our hermetic seal
each of us dancing
on

ON STARRY THIGHS

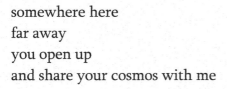

You open wide
on starry thighs
goddess
god
lover

somewhere here
far away
you open up
and share your cosmos with me

I become part of your spiraling dust
I am rock and ice
haunting echoes
of your pulsing lust

I breathe in your solar systems
I am asteroids and planets
flaring heat
of your sun rising eternal

I sink into your inky darkness
I am meteors and rings
orbiting hopes
of your uncharted universe

I share my cosmos with you
opening up
so close
that we are intertwined
I become your lover

god
goddess
my own starry thighs
opened wide

MEDICINE FLIGHTS

You are my medicine
Magic in my heart and soul wild medicine
Body medicine a cry from the ancient
Awakening me to possibilities that
Gods must have dreamed

You are my medicine
Have brought those dreams to life to light
The way along trods wild songs wild
Ways and the maps of my mind
Stirring me calling me

This morning I woke and you were still here
To hold kiss comfort fulfill me
When I awake in the morning
You will be landing at Gatwick
And my bed will be empty

Now that you're away
All I can smell is sweetcorn
On my fingers thighs lips
While your songs play on miles away

You left my window open
The breeze making me miss your touch
All the more
Your radiator body
Electric blanket arms

Winter has come on like a lover
Covering autumn leaves in mourning frost

With your body no longer covering mine
Nature had to blanket the land
An apology from the divine

That night you had been a hawk
Silken silver blue feathers and a beak
Penetrating me with your glossy black eyes

Run with me into the open fields
Barefoot on the wet grass
Toes kiss the open sky
Stare at the stars
And know what it means to be alive

Trees knew our skin
Cement our fleet feet
And honest under the clouds
You've helped me find a better way to live
To live
To love
You

You're somewhere over Wyoming
Soaring out of sight
But I can still close my eyes
Smell your sweat

Every once in a while
We can still be surprised
By the littlest things
Those things that still count
My flesh stings with the taste of you
I wear your marks with pride
Nothing to hide

No need for the shame
When I have a place in your world
Your inner retreat

Shivering I can still feel you inside me
Swelling pumping yearning
For release and so much more
In your arms I've touched forever
A sea beyond sex mind or body
Letting go
Seeing constellations never conceived

Can you still taste my blood in your mouth
My flesh under your nails
My hair locked your grasp
As I feel you now across the sea

I can still hear the beat
Of hooves leaves falling and the drums
Leading the way
A series of faerie lights
That hadn't been there the day before

The giant slumbered on
As we left our baggage in the glen
Coming out with open hearts
And glittering rings

Somehow
Across the oceans and differences
Two souls can meet
As they were meant to

The last evening you were cold
withdrawn
a storm front heading east

Tomorrow will come
As planes touch down
Another chapter to evolve
In our wanton wandering journey
Moving forward

Tomorrow will come
We will discover
Mad medicine
Spirit medicine
The new steps
That lies between us

Come to us
whirling out of pens and keys
pages on fire with your wit

Inspired
lit up as the sparks fly

Wells bubble over
as bodies are drenched

Sweat beading furrowed brows
expanding with light

    The ink dries up

    We cry out in longing for you

Breathing you in
four winds by four of the world

Turning to the mirror
our hearts flicker finally to life

For we hold inspiration
doulas of the creative mind

The leaves call out
once more to soar
reflected in the glass

FERI MAGIC: WILD MAGIC

Give me messy magic
Give me wild love
Give me the tears, sweat and cum of the Gods.
I refuse to pussyfoot
Around the pagan roots
Of my heart.
My faith is inclusive
A sea of sun
Bathing us all in the rose window of reality.
I see Goddesses orgasm
Gods fuck
Siblings dance hand in hand.
My Goddess
Is not a dangling god
With breasts glued on.
I will not
Worship
From afar.
I cherish my wildness
My integrated paths
My blue eyes wide with wonder.
Come dance with me
In open groves
And downtown orgies.
Dance with me
Lover, sister, brother, friend
Dance with me in this messy magic.
Breathe air
Tread soil
Swim deep
Gaze into the flame.

Drink in all possibilities
Not just the guise
No matter your path.
Find your truth
Make your faith
Four dimensional.
My hands are open
Arms ready
Waiting
For when you are called to my side
To ride
This wild magic.

PEACOCK DREAMING

I needed to spend
to spend
time in the center of I AM
I needed to be bare
I need to be bare

left hand magic
finds its way between my legs
between my breaths
two points forward
and three points towards the wrist
I twist
I fumble into the stars
towards I AM

he comes to me
he comes
peacock beauty
lord of the painted fan

he comes to me
he comes
Melek Ta'us
he comes

his claws dig into the heart of the planet
spinning gold
spinning iron

the tips of his eye-feathers dust the heavens with a smile
I can feel the heavens smiling
smiling and opening up their thighs

its eyes are lit with blue flame behind black iridescence
cold and inviting

I ride
I ride
I oh gods
I am impaled
weighing out the world
as the world rocks me into
into
I AM

eyes on me
waves on me
gills breathe deep
this
yes
this

I stand before him
tall as him
mighty as him
for I AM

I stand before him
my claws digging into the heart of the planet
spinning gold
spinning iron

the tips of my fingers
stretch and dust the heavens with a smile

I kiss him on the cheek
I kiss him on the cheek
and the candlelight flickers in the cave

left hand still at work
left hand
fumbling towards the stars

I pull myself up from the water
I dive into I AM
stopping to breathe in deeply
bare before a blue flame
bare before the candlelight

bare
there
before myself

bare

there
before myself

bare

before I AM

everywhere we think we go
crying understanding as it flows out blue
blue skinning her smile
mile by mile
lost as the trance dance into oblivion into tomorrow.

the biggest thief in life is time.

can't keep up with the pen want to record the blue
page by page
as the trance goes
on one fire out
one breath
breathing always against life or death
faces mask each revelation in the sheets.

sex is easy, love is harder.

again the storms come
in the end we each have our futures
cinderella at midnight
don't go don't go don't let the last shoe fall
just one last dance last trance into forever a dream
funny somehow it all makes more sense like this.

love is a precious thing
a startle at night
wondering if they're okay
an attempt to catch a star
putting together the story is what's hard.

death is easy, living is harder.

we're in this life to learn
remember
wave to wave
pull down the moon pull down the moon and she's there.

if we knew the future
we'd know what to do from the start
if we knew the future
we'd avoid the pain on the way there
wouldn't we?

it's strange the way
that the imperfections make the day
and in the end makes us what we are:
ourselves.

sometimes the deep amazement
the candlelight of passion expression
one touch to awaken us all
one touch to remember
something old, something blue.

Close your eyes.
Live for today.

THANKFUL TO BE FREE

I was always the one wrapped in black
silks and blacker velvet
you undid me bit by bit
laying me out in the golden light of flickering flame
crowning me

We were in our own bodies
powerful and strong
tanned and voluptuous
and you were in my body
I a slave to you
until you called me mistress
your love?

Now I've left my golden skin
undone myself bit by bit
for the snows fell outside
and I was gone
you have your own slave
mistress
love and I am merely myself

your murder takes flight
across skin and skies
awaiting
the next battle
between us

I open up the cabinet
and find you stored like knick knacks
on the shelf

Our hopes in the night
selected taxidermy tools

Our dreams of tomorrow
the shells collected by the sea

Our fears of separation
a jar of golden flakes

Our passions shared in secret
prayer shawls from forgotten lands

No one else comes to this cabinet
to see the world we created together

No one else comes to this cabinet
to dust off my forgotten hopes

Here in my kunstkammer
in my room of memory and obsession

A cabinet in the corner
opened now
missing you
missing you

AFFAIRS OF THE HEART

Our lips pushed
the moon into submission
waxing and waning
in a cloak of night
certain of what was to rise

How might I give recompense
for kisses shed
like leaves from a tree
as normal as nature
seasons in their time

How might I gain forgiveness
for nothing wronged
a sea of sensuality
embracing the waves
foam bobbing to the shore

Our time was
what it was meant to be
I will not bend
my bloodied knee
to beg in defense

We share a breath
a lament cast to the zephyr
heavens open wide
to our dissolution
our worlds
laid to waste

They burst forth
from empty thighs
the dreams and fears of our heart

You kissed me fiercely
not so long ago
you kissed me
forced your way in like fire
you kissed me
and I felt my spirit open up
not so long ago

They come screaming from me
horns and smiles
feral moans in the heavens
our sacred dreams gone awry

You told me nothing
not so long ago
you told me
that they would be your downfall
you told me
and I felt my spirit open up
not so long ago

They rip me up
leave me barren
the dreams and fears of our heart

What are our lips
but hungry saviors of the light?

You held onto me
not so long ago
you held me
ravaging my essence at every caress
you held me
and I felt my spirit open up
not so long ago

They destroy me
and leave me cold
feral moans in the heavens

What are our needs
but truths spoken in our bones?

They burst forth
Left me alive
The dreams and fears of our heart

inhaling our star dust
in the twilight of passion
eyes lock to eyes
with mumbled fear and longing

I open my heart
one page at a time
exposing my secret teachings
showing you chapters unwritten

fingers fumble and fly
pulling upon the lines
as bodies struggle
against our unspoken needs

holding fast our fantasies
we twist and turn
the fabric on your thighs
a veil between the worlds

let me open my mind
to the shape of YES
my lips quaking under a past
of knowing NO so well

in an ancient gasp
hips push up to the sky
the ground meeting heaven
paused for an eternity

silence speaks the name

of a time without words
my breath held
your cry ringing out

let us write down the words between us
let us clear the way
for a space between sighs
stars held together in the night

ELEMENT: SCENT

Spicy darkness
slides down
between my lips
as I breathe in
your heady fragrance
sweat and cedar
tangy aroma of of open skies

devouring

      every

            drop

BEYOND EGGSHELLS

I breathe deeply into the charge
of our daily lives
as if my breath carried
more than quaking words on the wind

Writing out the pros and cons
of journeys undertaken
I crumble inward
afraid of what I might find inside

Lessons and untouched hands
secrets whispered in code
spoken in the shade
a noonday sun behind the clouds

High in the sky along the river
cable cars pull us from the shore
out of the daily window
spying our own escape

Days drag by in echoing corridors
knitted and penned together
tears falling into a cup
for the tea leaf reader to discern

So I let the words flow out
turn the fun house mirror
flat as my voice
when the melancholy descended

Let me walk the borderline
telling myself along the way
beautiful lies
and awe inspiring truths

I walk the borderline
past eggshells and fragments
into who I may just be
into who I will become

Iowa & East

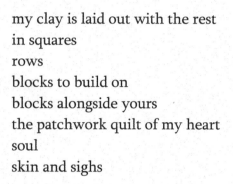

away from the sun
flying from the earth air water fire
fire burning bright
you soar
wings of a bird
high in my metamorphosphere
my change of pace

my clay is laid out with the rest
in squares
rows
blocks to build on
blocks alongside yours
the patchwork quilt of my heart
soul
skin and sighs

from my vantage I am myself
removed
clear
not the mirror of any others
where the ground and sky
blend in a bank of clouds
and my mind
is my own

from here the sun blazes
the river flows
the earth is a patchwork gown
the air keeps me afloat
flying away

flying east
away from the sun
my metamorphosphere
away from you
my change of pace

HOODED FALCON

I wait, hooded
Pull my eyes open
Lift me up
And let me soar

THE BOOK OF BONDS

...the world held in place

you slither into the space
between my passions
waking me from my erotic slumber
chains rattling at the sound of you

fibers twist and turn
between silken fingers
pushing up against my body
longing for your siren's touch

cold tiles test our knees
between rattled gasps
candles dancing in the darkness
painting shadows across our brow

from the floor you gaze
between needful kisses
my bindings winding tighter
with every no that cries out yes

scaled and squirming on the ground
between lines of jute
begging for tensions release
firm touch pulling deeper still

slide serpent formed into me
between starry thighs
I will take you for what you are
bound forever to my will

A SERVANT'S PRAYER

You lay
languidly back
as I lay out our course
nervous of what
you will think
of my tribute

Black latex
slides down
over each finger
snaps into place
as you look up
grant me a smile

Hands lube wet
palm to palm
in a lover's prayer
as eye catches eye
and I stop
to stare

I take you in
as one finger at a time
you take me
into your cavern
your secret realms
breath by breath

Clench and release
you make room for me
in your life

I coach you
on taking me in
taking this path together

Each grunt
builds on the last
until at last
you open up
rosebud
blooming in my palm

Birthing goddess
welcoming god
I stop caring
as my hand rests
inside your root
and comes alive

Pulse to pulse
my fingers
reach up
caressing eternity
in your churning core
from the inside

Both of our heads
roll back
tears streaming
clenching down
in time
with my heart

Let me worship
this moment

of vulnerability
bowing low
your servant
before the sling

Your spark inside
explodes
before my eyes
each breath
an eternity
in the thunderous sky

You writhe
divinity unfurling
quaking in my hands
rain streaming
down both
of our flushed cheeks

I pull away
moment at a time
until you release me
trying so desperately
to hold onto
this moment

Open wide, inside
your starry thighs
I am stripped away
as my hands
tremble at the loss

It poured like rivulets
down the small of backs
under arm pits
on upper lips
as we dive
dive
to the gold of our hearts
the alchemy of sweat

THE CAVERN PAINTING

Kiss me desert poet
who keeps the cave lit
Candles that beg
never return
Beautiful and terrible Lord

Show me the elegance
of sandstorm affairs
Hardened hands that cry
more oh more
Secret and sensual lover

Beyond the stone walls
where you fortify your heart
A rose rises
up from the sand
Into our heavy hands

I never spoke the tongue
that kissed my lips
Serpent sweet
snakes entwining
Our long hair entangled

Drying in the heat
of our remnants laid out
Our clothing clings onto
the shreds of yesterday
Sweetness scenting our form

Kiss me desert poet
who keeps the cave lit
Kiss me goodbye
never to return
Beautiful and terrible love

In the darkness
your relics rise
from the obscurity
of buried places I'd forgot
were masked from view

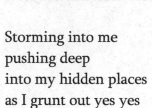

Storming into me
pushing deep
into my hidden places
as I grunt out yes yes
under my breath

Again and again
with tears falling
like a silent rain
my fertile pain
washing away in a rising tide

I lament
as you force your way
into my breath
crying out as I gasp for air
beneath the waves

Give me more
echoes in your pulse
let me shackle you
to the rock
of your own dread

Tie me to the rock
and let the Kraken come

Bind me to the rock
and let the eagles peck

Consign me to the rock
until Ragnarok roars

Tie me to the rock
and let me drown

GRUDGE

You kiss me
petals blooming on ravenous lips
the venom of your resentment
stinging me
as we stumble into bed

Passion flows out of us
for what are lust and rage
but dancing cousins
caught up in the same steps
on the ballroom floor

Hands grabbing hair
fangs digging to bone
hope clinging to your sweat
as we dream
of a time before spittle and fear

My nails find purchase
skin singing out in suffering
our hardships unfolded
between sweaty sighs
across the tangled sheets

Let it spill
let us remember tomorrow
nourished roots erupting
into the towering fronds
of our forgiveness

I love how you
slide in and out
of all
my holes
a man with more
possibilities
for you to enter
my body
my heart

INWARD

teasing me
I push myself up
towards your waiting flesh

without doubt
you glide in
my head rolling back

rapture breaks
across my brow
pulling you close

ecstatic breath
filling me up
with each thrust

we surrender
sweat pouring down
our fiery forms

diving inward
the frenzy rises
hearts beating as one

endorphin high
my eyes squint with the pleasure
as quick hand presses slightly and penetrates my flesh
mouth dry my moan
cunt sobbing throbbing rolling against the table beneath me
    one
        at
        a
    time
in starbursts
the flashes catching candle and lamp
the thrusts cause my hips to rise as I bite my lip
drawing virgin blood lost long ago
now they are drawn together an aria of pain and pleasure
grasping for the table
hands sweat as does my face legs breasts heaving
as the lace is wrapped about me
the satin pulling at the wounds
endorphin high
the tears roll down
as he pulls out
    one
        at
        a
    time
and I collapse in exhaustion

HIGH SHINE

You caress
my second skin
tanned by a process
that has left me changed

You penetrate
my shielded spirit
battered by a life
that has left me bruised

Polish me
to a high shine
my love
a high shine

Let me reflect
upon my journey
my love
upon my journey

You massage
my exposed hide
scraped and scarred
that lets me be guarded

You infiltrate
my bare being
vulnerable and trembling
as you see me unveiled

As you polish me
to a high shine
my love
a high shine

Each strike
lands
in a cascade
of crimson

Raising my wand
with each spell
you push back
into me

Lines like ogham
fate read
in the red
of your flesh

Fine Rattan
flies with fury
Bamboo snapping
as it descends

Koa wood
a prayer to the gods
Birch calling
tradition home

Tools laid bare
you become
Oak and Ash
Willow and Thorn

I trace our fate

as you sigh
following you
into the trance

Each howl
each moan
a sacred moment
echoes forth

Catalyst / Catharsis

Leather lashes
my salacious flesh
beating
in
time
with our questing hearts

Sweat pouring
down heavenly bodies
drumming
out
the noises
around us

Magician in black leather
Priest draped in desire
beat me down
into
the truths
called mystery

Let me hold open
the sacred gateway
screaming
each
moan
to the eternal

Set the rhythm
and ride my hide

to the other side
of the veil

MANGOES

You are dripping down my chin again
though I have not seen you in months
a dream cast in fresh spices and honeyed wine
succulent sweet
your sweat lapped up by my tongue
nails dug into tender flesh
chains and canes thumping across your skin
bent and bowed before my boots
a willow in the dimmed light

Feral growls erupt from your throat
fangs dig in to find a pulse and latch on
breathing my ghostly apparition away
candle lit and heady in my maw
eyes locked in the shade
of your long and limber branches
mango filling my senses
spinning into dream

MOLTEN

Let me wash up on your blackened shores
take in your burning glory
cling to your molten remains

Confessions fall from weary limbs
as you pull upon my heartstrings
aching from years at sea

I bear witness to your dancing waves
walk to the edge of fear
grateful for your love

Push me down into your belly
drape me in your smoldering grace
dive down into your core

We have been here before
crashing up against the rocks
of our desire to be free

Spin us out into the darkness
hold tight our stony truths
Let me grasp
      tight
           no more

IMPRESSION

You've left your impression here on my skin
from your hand residing dutifully beautifully in mine
and it shall never wash away

those lips
silken petals that traced their way across neck
cheek
leaving meek scars where they came to rest
speaking volumes not only of poetry oaths divinity
but silent subtle belonging

hundreds have come before me
they too seeking the essence in your eyes
but with me you opened those orbs
you looked out to see

mark my life line with our aging together
my love forever embedded in your smile
your stare
your hair brushing across your shoulders
through my fingers
soft strands velvet on my palm

You've left your impression here on my skin
not with a ring or a brand
not with bites or cuts nor binding oaths
but by your hand resting dutifully beautifully in mine
and the fact that your flesh is my own

COME DAWN

Kiss me by the first rays of sun falling upon my tender flesh

Ravage me by the casting gaze of the brutal moon

Orbit me with your lips pressed courageously on mine

We are the planets whirling through the space between us

We are the meteors showering the world with our delight

Cast your lot upon our astrological charts written in the stars

Tear down the lines between us with a ravenous caress

We are the comets streaming our tears across a blackened sky

We are the asteroid fields of uncertain passion crowded 'round

Hurl me against the walls of your blessed permission

Miss me when we part come the fall of morning light

TRANSLUCENCE

Cast a circle
and roll me down
pouring yourself into
the shell
between us

MY PRECIOUS

I cling to you
my golden ring etched
with the ancient poem

Twisting you on
I become invisible
as a breath, a gasp

Let me be
your precious you said
as I lay down

Your lap my bower
your lips my journey
away from green pastures

Years later I twist
turn the golden ring
in my palm

Unable to throw you
in the fire
on the mount

Unable to put you
back on
my old comfort

My precious
your precious

forever
no more

CRIMSON

Oxblood gems
rattle in my chest
a slowly
settling
smile

Staining my teeth
with the color
of your lies
you are pulpy
sweet

Welts rise up
gore and passion
anger holds
no more
today

I dig into denial
shake my fist
kiss away
ignorance
tears

Ruby knuckles
bloody with fear
consume
my resentment
lust

Let me be
tomorrow's fallacy
sinking
out of
love

SLEEPING TOGETHER,
FALLING APART

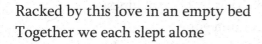

You were sleeping on one side of your pain
Curled up with suffering like a pillow

Racked by this love in an empty bed
Together we each slept alone

Turning to the space between us
Hands reach out into the loneliness

We fought with each stroke
Devouring furious kisses on a hunger strike

What shape is misery in this lust
Erupting in a howl of empathy

Breasts and hands struggle in the dark
Enemies on each side of the sheets

Rushing through solitude in your company
Sumptuous stars spinning on their heels

We become our own callous conclusion
Forgiveness forgotten with every turn

UPON THE WAVES

You are silver lines
Baited breath drawn back and forth across time.
You are a dangling poem
Left with words still writ upon the stars.

There are some forms of love that feel like madness
Contagious I breathe and feel him gone
Afraid to breathe out lest others catch this thing I have
Don't have.

In the harbor my madness is docked
Silence, simple silence
No voice, no words
Sails slack
A diet that atrophied the line down to a trickle
convinced me
Somehow
It would be alright.

But then the wind
The gust
One message
Blowing me back out to sea.

I feel you in my stomach, in my heart.
I can feel your heat against the back of my neck.
I can feel you standing in my spine.
The winds whip
Storms churn
Lightning striking on my lips.

Contracts released

Words proclaimed
Space made clean
They are not enough to let you go.

And then the wind dies
As surely as it began
Because you are not here
Never could be here
Here at my side.

Untangle lines
Come clean once more.
Come clean and sail once more into port.

A few years
A few lifetimes
Longing for the open sea
Longing to cross the ocean and find new lands
But our storms would sink us both
Dancing as we drown.

You are silver lines
Baited breath drawn back and forth across time
You are a dangling poem
Empty waves waiting for your glistening caress.

THE BOOK OF KEYS ⚷

...the world unlocked

THE OFFERING

(for Odin)

Black winged glory
raven delirium
knocks loose the moon

Seasons push free
the eternal growth
of gnarled oak

From a planted seed
dreaming madness takes hold
reaching towards the sky

Climb the mighty world tree
roots flowing with wandering wraiths
reflecting our timeless branches

Hang me from your powerful trunk
take me into inspiration
seeking our immortal light

Eternity licks the desert dry
curving hips of mother's bones
catching every drop of blood

Ankle pierced and dangling
let me be carved for wisdom
ready to receive the waiting well

Fill me with frantic song
My warrior wit
Thankful in it's travels

Peck open my eyes
leave me blind no more
the night unfolding before us

SHAKE FREE THE MOORINGS

Dance me a web of stars
thighs spread wide beneath my wings
feathers falling across your licorice curls
tangled between moans

The sky shuddered
shook free its moorings
sailed into the night

Breathe in the musk of yesterday
devour tomorrow's desperate strokes
decadence in emerald and turquoise
wrapping myself around you

The sky shuddered
shook free its moorings
sailed into the night

Spin me a net of burning gems
arms welcoming my beating marrow
with iron eyes and heart of jet
innocent with every taste

The sky shuddered
shook free its moorings
sailed into the night

Lunge into my taloned hands
camped around your burning flame
powerful in freedom's flight
galaxies twisting 'round my heart

The sky shuddered
shook free its moorings
sailed into the night

Collapse into my nothingness
of days before a rising sun
lips locking as we pull close the wind
angels singing in the dark

The sky shuddered
shook free its moorings
sailed into the night

My languid lover
mother of the ivory egg
mirror touched spread starry thighs
whirling out the dreams of life

You are my shuddering sky
shaking free the moorings of desire
sail me oh sail me
                into the night

i remember you
my eyes locked in rapture
as you took the stage

tweed clung to my thigh
like a famished lover
devouring each sigh

as we gathered
you cleared your throat
and i could not look away
aldous
aldous

i remember
the magic you painted
that I could never have

i remember me
three nights later
tears streaming down

tweed clung to my thigh
like a desperate man
afraid to let go

i let go

of it all

cold water clung to my thigh
cold water clung to my skin
i drifted down
and for some reason
thought of you

aldous
what a strange memory
to end on
of sitting around you

not the memory of his screams
not my mother
not the tears
not the sorrow

aldous
it was you
with my last breath

i was wide eyed in wonder
breathing in life
three hours

three days before the end
three wishes made true

let me dance
let me know
let me elate

and i had

the last two at your feet

when water rushes in
it chokes
then presses down

swallow me aldous
swallow me whole
take me down your lanes of dream
to where I danced
but never tasted

swallow me aldous
swallow me deep
take me past cacti and mushroom
to where you danced
and my heart will call it home

love

in the end
love

not the gnawing anguish
not years of malaise
mixed with stifling depression

in the end
love

and you
and you

BELOVED OF DUNG

Kiss me
Khepri
He who has come into being

Kiss me
Hard shelled
Scarab-bodied ancient one

Roll the sun
Over me
Let me be the sky alive

Transform me
Molding my heart
Self-created like you

I am Nut
Swallowing you whole

I am Nut
Mother of your hungry mandible

Crawl from me
Kiss me
As I moan in your wake

(for Persephone)

You are leaving me
my love
as you always do

The frost on your lips
is melting
climbing towards the light

Being married to me
my love
takes strength and grace

Black veils and shadow
icy realms
death and mourning cries

Each year you come to me
my love
and each year you have to go

A step at a time you leave
my love
my realm empty without you

The cherry blossoms fall
a flurry
falling on my fiery heart

YOUR ANVIL

(for Hephaestus)

Sweating brow
pumping away
at the billows
in the balefire of life

Let me grab
onto the scruff
of your wild beard
my iron pounding beloved

I shift beneath
your mighty body
taking you in
as I sing out your flame

Your dust and dirt
cling to me
alabaster skin
turning grey under your hips

TREE OF KNOWLEDGE

(for Lilith)

Straddling
first born
fruit in hand
we moan together

Hips writhe
flesh on flesh
shadow and light
in the desert

Inside me
sacred tree
throne carved out
of your inner secrets

Slide in
third gendered
lover of the hidden
lover of open thighs

Slide out
forbidden dream
a history played out
remembered

My arms wrap
around the nothing
of the space between us

Spaces
paces away
you breathe me
into your prayers

How do we
open up
into the veins
of our desire
you ask

I bare my neck
and bear your fangs
slipping in

NAGA

Their skin flickers against mine
Wet with sweat and juices sweet
As flames soar up around
Undulating serpent

Kissed of brands and fiery hair
Scaled and stained
Ze writhes its way in
Tongue to tongue
Chest to chest

As you curl up
In this warm place
Twisting and turning to find a home
Here in my gaze

Let the Dead Part Ways

I taste you wet on my skin
I taste you shadowy river lapping at my mind
You pass through me
Over me
Under me
I taste you wet on my skin

You pass through me as you pass through Turkey
Become Firat
You pass through me as you pass through Iraq
Become al-Furat
You pass through me as you pass through Syria
Become Prath
I taste you wet on my skin

You are many tongued
Lapping at my mind
Perth
Yep'rat
Euphrates
I taste you wet on my skin

Kiss me sister of Tigris
Kiss me shining blackness and palm fronds
I taste you wet on my skin
I taste you shadowy river lapping at my mind
You pass through me
Over me
Under me
I taste you wet on my skin

I am wet with you
I am wet with your kisses
I am soaked through
Leannan the Living
Leannan of Earth
Of dust
Of dirt
Of fur and cum
I am soaked through

I am wet with you
I am wet with your kisses
I am soaked through
Leannan the Dead
Leannan of Water
Of tears
Of blood
Of moans and sighs
I am soaked through

We part here
Leannan and Leannan
Living and Dead
Earth and Water
Dust and tears
Dirt and blood
We part ways here
For we are soaked through
And she paddles away

I taste you wet on my skin
I taste you shadowy river lapping at my mind
You pass through me
Over me

Under me
You pass through me
and I taste you wet on my skin

VICTOR

(for Victor and Cora Anderson)

You hold my hand across the veil,
drenching my spirit in wisdom.

We are the stuff that stars are made of.
I open my eyes to a truth

Ten pointed mysteries, wrap around me
Ruby, iron, pearl and beyond.

Let me lock lips with your beauty.
Fill my being with all you hold to light.

Black is your innocent heart
as I laugh up every illuminated morsel.

I dipped my toe into the wetness
feeling myself, dive down into the waves

Splashing then swimming. I caress the water
longing for each drop on my skin.

Blossoms bloom; into my eternal power
shining a smile from the infinite flame.

GUARDIAN OF WISDOM

(for Black Mother)

I feel your icy hands
talons digging into my spine
blink me dry
with the thousand eyes of a venomous mother

Open up your craving mouth
devour me with every touch
toxic caresses
deep within the cave

Bare my chest
blood beating in a thunderous noise
screaming out loud
in dripping crimson

Wrap me in shadowed sighs
open me up to your ravishment
signs of coming horror
mutilation of our dreams

Hooves stamp in the world below
echoing in my bones
as I dance I dance
into your icy hands

I shall spin into your hungry maw
to rend my cowardice and despair
stripping me clean
black heart burning bright

STONEBREAKER

(A call to Gugalanna, Bull of Heaven)

Monster in my bones
Beloved of my first tears
I hear you breaking stones
I hear you breaking stones
In my heart

Gugalanna in my bones
Bull of Heaven in Kur
I claim the fear and woes
I claim the fear and woes
In my heart

I battle monsters
Each day
I battle you my sweet
Each day
I battle my reflection
Each day
In the shadowed lands of Kur

Monster in my bones
Beloved of my first tears
I hear you breaking stones
I hear you breaking stones
In my heart

You flow
blue from your lips
into the crown
of the world
a well
filled with potential

Two spinning
in the night
brother to brother
sister to sister
lover to lover
children
of the stars

Open me up
to your mysteries
to the truths
of the rose above
of the sea below
lands between
each breath

I pull open
my spirit
to let you in
let you in
divine twins
inspiration
for my hunger

The trance
of four eyes
catch mine
four feathers
falling across my brow
four hands
four dancing feet

Two bobbing cocks
two wet cunts
two holy wells
filled
with potential
standing before me

From the stars
up to my lust
into the essence
into the crown
blue from your lips
you flow

Fir I

Pour down a cascade of snow
fall over my evergreen desires
flutter your whiteness against my branches
bury me under your weight
I will bend to you but will not break

Fir II

I will moan out your name
as you melt yourself down into my roots
sustain me with your wetness
fill me up drop by drop

Fir III

Come the height of summer you will be gone
my parched lips needful of your caress
burning under a wrathful sky

Fir IV

Pour me down with a deluge of lust
kissing me hard for every day missed
the mist holding us together
I stand tall beneath you
as we rattle the world between us

1,000 PIECES

(for Isis)

You found me
scattered across the land
lost
to myself
and the world

You found me
and gathered me up
hope
breathing in
as you searched

You found me
one thousand pieces
torn
in rage
by our brother

You found me
except for one
piece
beast eaten
in his belly

You found me
and laid me out
shreds
of myself
in your arms

You found me
mud of the Nile
gathered
phallus made
shaped with love

You found me
penetrating yourself
love
breathing out
as you moaned

You found me
cumming over me
clay
hardening deep
in your body

You found me
each day found
thousands
of pieces
plus this one

You find me
striding across the land
lost
to us all
never again

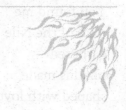

glistening black wraps 'round her hips
drums beating in the whispered night
dancing blind before the stars
with opened heart

opened up she touched the sky
sighing deep in shared delight
laughing clear with each caress
and riding high

riding high the flames leapt higher
water flows through pulsing veins
lapping at the ancient dreams
the goddess smiles

smiling wide with legs spread wider
kneeling over hungry earth
dancing towards immortal love
a primal cry

primal cry that rings out clear
matted hair of mud and grass
sparks flying up towards heaven's might
fused as one

fused as one by skin and bone
fur and spit and cum and tears
let loose the dawn of hearts alight
embracing true the glistening black

EARTHLY LOVE

Your mountains rose up from quake after quake
Pangaea becoming your molten needs that lifted your hips
Into my soaring sky

My winds danced across your thorny bushes and soaring pines
Whispering my desires into lush green and clinging vines
That wrapped around my breath

Laying beneath me so close and yet so far away
Chasms that long for my storms to plunge your abyss
Just as your towering cliffs invade my midnight desires

Each night the sun sets and you see me oh you see me full of
glory
Lit with a web of pearls crying oh come to me lover
Come to me love and fill me deep

Deep as your ocean eyes
Deep as your running river lips
Deep as your endless iron heart
Deep as your valley mysteries
Deep as you my love
Deep as you

Open up and spread my starry thighs
Watching me give birth to a new horizon with each thrust
Feeling me sing a solar system with every moan

Pin my clouds against you in a fog
Let me rustle your leaves with each kiss
My quivering tsunamis laying to waste your endless vistas

Call me your endless night as you pull me down on top of you
Sand storms rising up to greet me
Lightening erupting from my shaking overhead

My endless earthen lover
Caves and bone
I shall straddle you forever
As we clutch one another
In storm and peace
And love

THE BOOK OF RECONCILIATION

...the world found anew

RECONCILIATION

Fingers tipped in gold
forgiveness comes
a thousand versions strong
rallying in the rivers
of ancient scars

Heal me over
white lines
buried at the water's edge

Win me over
teach me compassion
for my conquerors
liberated
in this whitewash
of the heart

-TO WHOMEVER PAINTS IT, COLORS ME THEIRS-

across a dream
crossed by screams
I call for you to ride away from your complacency
Ride the waterways of my body
Your hands stern but soft would row the way
Along my valley
Waters
Lakes
Streams
Past the rapids of my heart
Into the vast ocean of my soul

let me sing your mind
your tongue
paint my sweat upon your brow
bind you in my acrylics
watercolors
pastels
and the lyrics of my life

be my palette
let me brush you across my flesh
let my skin

tell the tales
of our loving

the roofs here are blood brown
colors of stagnancy in a sunset
sunrise paint box
we shall paint our house purple red
fuchsia white
and let our children know
all the colors of creation

let me not be watercolor to wash off
let me be your india ink

blending blurring knotting swirling
painting a dream
along the waterways of our life

LIVING THE SHOW

Here is a toast to the rebels and visionaries who know what it is to be a performer.

Words projected out to the humbled ears of waiting crowds as I become my own poem, projected.

The container of my art transforms into a place my heart can spring forth, ready to be vulnerable.

If all things are permissible in the name of the sacred or the stage, what happens after the curtains fall?

I struggle for my lines and cannot find the voice for improv in the roaring world called life.

The curtain rises and I raise a toast to everyone brave enough to stand before the lights.

When the performance comes to an end, I will take my bow and thank you all.

For holding space.

For holding me.

EVERY LINE

teases and travails
lay out the smoldering heat
of your need
face to face
in a single breath
emerald lines
clinging to your eyes
as palms and psalms
sing of love for a moment
until I unbind you
and mourn every line

you are will never be what you need they need anyone needs
crunching fists and bloody blades
fear drips down like childhood
empty bottles empty lives an empty life like mine
so full too full filled up with all of it all of it
bursting damn of lies and forgotten memories
crimson cracks the window
haul me screaming away
can't leave won't leave the temptation
a train a car speeding by gripping the rail
it echoes keeps echoing a whispered chasm cacophony
i echo keep echoing words stale on my tongue
desperate for something I can't find
won't find will never find
gasping
rocking
nails digging in
breathing in
hold hold hold hold hold hold hold hold

    release

        tasting the silence
        between each tear

DREAMS ALIGNED

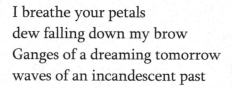

Serpent dancing
closing into the dark
in this date with myself

I breathe your petals
dew falling down my brow
Ganges of a dreaming tomorrow
waves of an incandescent past

Breathe the falling truths
of sweaty dance halls and ancient temples
my temples wet with your perspiration

I feel the web of my spoken sentience
lit with the stars of morning dew
mourning you no more

Dance into my limbs a longing lover
my toes wiggling in your dampness

Dance into my hungry hips
undulating in your earthly arms

Branches sway from sun above to moon below
stars and roses alight with our brilliance

Folding the flame of our possibility
my fingers hold the heat but do not burn

I will not burn

I will close into the dark
date myself
with years spent and years to cum

Years to come under
my own eyes open and bound
three in one earthly body

I will drip wet and spin high
on blades and waves of eternity

Sing me sweet moan
drum me out a rhythm

Breathe in my petals
dew flowing down
I will drown you with your gills wide open

Open wide and find inside yourself the stars I see there
dare to open your eyes
temples held behind lashed lids
the words of wetted shadows rolling down

Drown

Open your gills in the dark
in the light
in the dawn of shadow breath
reborn in the roots of tomorrow's past

Open your gills in the dark
serpent dancing
dating yourself
with every wave

HEART BY DARKNESS

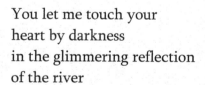

You let me hear your
heart by darkness
through the still water
of the river

Down to the dock
we walk the stairs
your feet
have touched a thousand
times and a thousand more
generation upon generation
of family
of you
etched into
the wood

You let me touch your
heart by darkness
in the glimmering reflection
of the river

Standing on the dock
porcupine quills
in our ears
and scallops alive once more
showing your pride
to me
as I melt

within
my stony
self

You let me see your
heart by darkness
by the lapping sighs
of the river

We leave the docks
and paddle into
the past
through childhood joy
and the raising of a boy
who would someday
say to me
yes
yes this
yes

By the light of day
I let my tongue loose
unchecked and boundless
and you said to me:

*yes this
yes

I'm that boy
grown, on that water
to say YES
with you*
so I say yes
to the river
to the river
yes to the river and to you

This is
my year by the sea
pen in hand
as I work through
the hard places
of my heart

Coming to visit
my friends say
I look happy
for the first time in ages
while with pot of tea raised
I shake inside

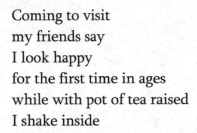

Patterns in sand
come and go
as I wander
the beaches
looking for hope
a place to sit
to wait out the storm

Wringing my hands
half-smiling at strangers
I breathe
practicing the gifts
of the time to be spent
here

So fetch me some madeleines
and my wool derby hat

fetch me a notebook
some ink and a desk
let me set up residence
in this space by the shore
as the waves come in
come out
to find me

This is
my year by the sea
pen in hand
as I work through the hard places
of my heart

REPRISE

Collecting my sighs
outside the monoliths of 1st avenue
I finger wounds
processing forgotten prayers
plastered on the inside of my skin

Snow storms rise up
a flurry flickering across my face
coldness from my stony breast
while you keep your head down
and try to just take the next step

Fears and fragility
coalesce under your tender lips
melting away my sorrow
sticking to boots left at the door
of our two bedroom reprise

Streaming tears
I offer you a safety until spring
when I will collect from you
my red loomed shawl
and our next move towards freedom

Pale eyes meet
with bodies bundled up tight
to brush back my hair
kissing my brow with certainty
that I will return once more

MOTHER

Softness
tickles my nose
paws wrapped around
my devoted form

She waits for me
For I am Hers.

I hold myself up
a self-referential gesture
to examine
this thing
I am
       I am

my identities clash
become a single storm
in the night

across the city
away from the drag
of our daily lives
you let me peer in
into you
into myself

we are cut from moans
truths of a cryptic flame
homes and observation

dimensions unfold
height width depth
time and tone
the bones
of our ancestors
crying out

outside the brown-out
inside candles flutter
finding myself in the dark

thunderous cracks
cross over
into consciousness
wiping free clutter
lightning and hail
held in my hands

the mirror held high
vying for my attention
at the eye of the storm

a gift of dreams
opens my heart
gills breathe deep
breathing into
I am
        I am

GRACE

In my body
they pushed inside like a wave
thinking they'd touched me
where it matters

I lowered my shoulders
lower myself down
show them no fear
and the waters fall
they fell
fell from grace

Buried in the catacombs
of my earthen tread
I walk on
casting aside memories
memoirs featuring their name

I gather up the tomes
treaties and treatments
and hold each one up
to the light
burning bright
in my veins

The darkest nights
can come to define
the brightest days
a cool breeze
blowing through
my uncertainty

Turning over
my wrists and arms
I find myself
more than the sum
of my scars

I cannot unweave
the warp and weft
of this tapestry
I cannot unremember
lines cut in
as the music played on

So instead I dance
spin the spiral loom
cast myself into the kiss
of loving myself
and all my past

Forgiving myself

So often
the hardest step

Join me in the dance
join me as we whirl
and twirl
our journey back
journeying back
to grace

BLESSED AND SCARRED

Whether under dark of moon or shining sun
energy runs deep between our whispered gasps

Bodies throw wide the gates
of needful deity and throbbing spirit
ready for all that comes our way

I don't mind the splinters as you call forth the Green Man
the pebbles under my knees for the Goddess
my scraped up skin
or our scraped up hearts

Crimson and nude
verdant green and silken blue
we rise
we rise

Holy
sacred
powerful imperfect beings
beyond measure

CUP AFTER CUP

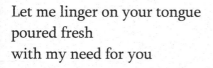

The scent
of espresso in the air
floods me with your fingertips
pressing down
on plastic
metal
grounds
and my lips

Let me linger on your tongue
poured fresh
with my need for you

Invite me down your throat
welcome me in
to recharge your spirit

Drink me in
creamy and sweet
hazelnut and rich roast

The scent of my grandfather's home
The smell of your breath each morning
The taste of our loving
our loving
cup
after
cup

BARE

the world
does not need
my every truth
packaged up
for easy consumption

let me
reclaim
myself
from before
your hungry eyes

i open my story
bare
and delete page
after
page

COAGULA

You are the last gasp of the incredible
guru of a thousand desperate breaths
coagulating in my heart

Laughter mirrors your branches and roots
digging down with chisel and claws
into the earth beneath our feet

Black winged fascination
I became myself in the safe space
of this uncertainty

Kiss the secret comforts of my tongue
become my cartel of compassion
know the shape of my every longing

Grant me safe passage
through the poetry in lyrical motion
into the sea of my own identities

I wrap you up in my arms
finding myself
clutching
myself

Fear falls away in an ocean of dream
passes wild between my parched lips
opening my story breath by breath

Lay down with me on the lava rocks
let me crawl into your hospital bed
let our hands cling tight
laying side by side.
We will share whispers
where only the lighting will hear us
and the world will rush by.

UNFINISHED

Stumbling
over me
I am not ready
for distribution

I am
An unfinished metaphor
of the heart
lines that trace wisdom through time

I become your broken kōan
your uncertain allegory

Paraphrase me over the years
unable to make sense of my stories

Let me be your tangled prose
your tortured parables

I am
unready
but that does not matter

So out I go
into the night

unready
unfinished

CREATION

I fuck myself
into the beauty
that I know is within

Go fuck yourself
becomes a prayer
that no one else knows

Starry thighs
mirror mine
carve the world anew

Starry thighs
mirror yours
carve the world anew

Eyes roll back
cries erupt
stars fly across the sky

Eyes open wide
our future unfolds
in each stroke of

creation

THIS GOD

Who is this rose above me
This god that is I AM
dove of love
daemon's spark
I would know myself in all my forms

Who is this mantle over me
This god that burns I AM
wisdom's sigh
eyes of Sophia
I would know myself in all my truths

Who is this egg surrounding me
This god that touches I AM
entrusted aura
caressing soul
I would know myself in all my shapes

Who is this flesh around me
This god that kisses I AM
beautiful skin
forces alive
I would know myself in all my power

Who is this flame within me
This god that burns I AM
passion alive
fueling drive
I would know myself in all my bliss

I AM

...and so are you

ABOUT THE AUTHOR

Lee Harrington is an internationally known spiritual and erotic authenticity educator, gender explorer, eclectic artist and award-winning author and editor on human erotic and sacred experience. He's been traveling the globe (from Seattle to Sydney, Berlin to Boston), teaching and talking about sexuality, psychology, faith, desire and more, who is grateful for the journeys and love he has found along the way. His many books include *Sacred Kink: The Eightfold Paths of BDSM and Beyond* and *More Shibari You Can Use: Passionate Rope Bondage and Intimate Connection*, and has been blogging about sex, spirit and energy since 1998. His podcast, blog, books, tour schedule and essay work can be found at www.PassionAndSoul.com.

As a poet, Lee's work has been published since the late 90s, appearing in such anthologies as *Queen of The Great Below: An Anthology in Honor of Ereshkigal* (Bibliotheca Alexandrina), *Spirals & Shards: Pagan Poetry from the Back of the Heart* (Asphodel Press), *Between The Lines* (Edmonds CC Press), *Dark*

Moon Rising: Pagan BDSM and the Ordeal Path (Asphodel Press), and *Sacred Power, Holy Surrender: Living a Spiritual Power Dynamic* (Alfred Press). He is a spirit worker whose devotion is dedicated to the goddess Bear, with deep roots in a variety of traditions, as shown in the book in your hands. His work as a sacred sexuality author, poet, photographer and painter can be found at www.TempleOracle.com.